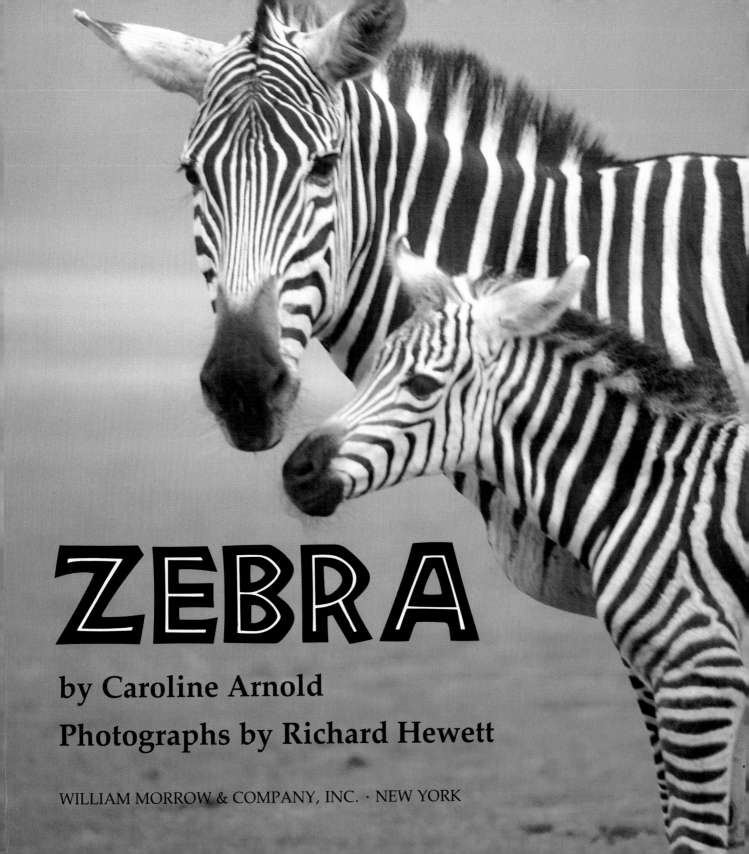

ZEBRA

by Caroline Arnold

Photographs by Richard Hewett

WILLIAM MORROW & COMPANY, INC. · NEW YORK

PHOTO CREDITS: Permission to use the following photographs is gratefully acknowledged: Caroline Arnold, pages 8–9; Eliot Brenowitz, pages 12, 31; Ron Garrison, San Diego Zoo, page 13.

Library of Congress Cataloging-in-Publication Data. Arnold, Caroline. Zebra. Includes index. Summary: Discusses the characteristics and habits of zebras and describes the life of a new little zebra at a large open-air wildlife park in New Jersey.   1. Zebras—Juvenile literature.   2. Six Flags Great Adventure Safari Park (N.J.)—Juvenile literature. [1. Zebras.   2. Six Flags Great Adventure Safari Park (N.J.)]
I. Hewett, Richard, ill.   II. Title.
QL737.U62A76 1987   599.72′5   87-1503   ISBN 0-688-07067-1 I ISBN 0-688-07068-X (lib. bdg.)

ACKNOWLEDGMENTS

We want to thank the Six Flags Great Adventure Safari Park in Jackson, New Jersey, for the opportunity to photograph the zebras in this book. We are grateful to all the park personnel who cooperated with us in this project, and in particular we thank David Barnes, Senior Supervisor of Animal Care, for his time, cheerful assistance, and expert advice. We also thank Angela Hewett and John Levin for all their help, and our editor, Andrea Curley, for her continuing enthusiasm and support.

THE tiny striped zebra struggled to stand on wobbly legs, leaning on his mother's warm belly for extra support. The baby's fur was still damp where his mother had licked him, and his eyes blinked in the early morning light. He had been born just a few hours earlier and was not yet used to life in the zebra herd.

The little zebra was the newest zebra at the wild animal park in New Jersey where he lived. Here he would grow up in the company of giraffes, antelopes, and other animals native to the African plains. In the park, as in the wild, these grass-eating animals share the same living space.

In Africa, the Swahili name for zebra is *punda milia,* meaning "striped donkey." Even though the zebra is not a donkey at all, one of the keepers at the park decided to name the new little zebra Punda. He was one of eight young zebras that had been born that summer.

Zebras and wildebeests, Ngorongoro Crater, Tanzania

Far away in Africa, thundering herds of wild zebras roam over the central, eastern, and southern plains. These herds, which sometimes combine to form groups of five hundred or more, are constantly moving across the broad grasslands in their search for food and water. Behind them lurk lions, wild dogs, and other meat-eating animals that depend on zebras for their food.

For Punda, finding enough food or escaping from dangerous hunters will never be a problem. He is fed a healthy diet, and the only people he is ever likely to see will be the animal keepers and park visitors.

Every day during the summer, and

on weekends in spring and fall, thousands of people come to the park to see the zebras and other animals. They drive through the park in cars, small trucks, and buses. There they see many kinds of animals roaming free in large enclosures and living much as they do in the wild. Although the zebras in the park have become used to having people nearby, they are not tame and do not like to be touched or handled. Even the keepers, who know the zebras well, are careful around them, for an angry or frightened zebra can kick or bite.

People have always been fascinated by zebras. Long ago, these animals were exhibited in ancient Rome. In the third century, the Roman emperor Caracalla trained zebras to pull a chariot. In Africa in the eighteenth and nineteenth centuries, European settlers used zebras for riding and as work animals. Like the native Africans, the Europeans also hunted zebras for food and for their beautiful striped skins.

Like horses, wild asses, and donkeys, zebras belong to the animal group with the scientific name *Equus*, which means "horse" in Latin. Today there are three different kinds, or species, of zebras, and they differ from each other in size, the number of stripes on their bodies, and the shape of the head. The three species of zebras are not directly related to each other, and they do not breed with one another.

Grévy's zebra

Grévy's zebra is the largest of the three species. It was named after the French president Jules Grévy, who was given a gift of such a zebra in 1882 by the emperor of Ethiopia. Grévy's zebra stands about 5 feet (1.5 meters) at the shoulders and weighs between 780 and 950 pounds (354–432 kilograms). Its head has large rounded ears and is similar to that of a mule. Its call, like the mule's, is a loud bray. The narrow black stripes of Grévy's zebra are nearly vertical and are more numerous than the stripes on other zebra species. It lives in dry semidesert areas of northern Kenya, Somalia, Ethiopia, and the Sudan.

There are two kinds of mountain zebras, the rare Cape mountain zebra and the slightly larger Hartmann's mountain zebra. This is the smallest zebra, standing only about 4 feet (1.2 meters) tall and weighing about 600 pounds (273 kilograms). Its shape is more like that of a wild ass, with a short, plump head and long, pointed ears. The stripes of the mountain zebra differ from those of other zebra species on the rump near the tail. There a series of small stripes forms a gridiron pattern across the spine.

The hooves of the mountain zebra are smaller and narrower than those of the other zebras. They are ideally suited for walking in the dry, stony mountains and hills where it lives in South Africa. Because of overhunting by early European settlers, the mountain zebras are in danger of extinction. Most now live either in protected reserves or in Mountain Zebra National Park in South Africa.

Hartmann's mountain zebra

Grant's zebra

The most numerous and widespread species of zebra, and the species most often seen in zoos and circuses, is the Burchell's, or plains, zebra. It is found in the open plains and grassy woodlands throughout East Africa.

Because Burchell's zebras that live in different areas have slight variations in markings, they have been divided into several subspecies. These include Grant's, Chapman's, and Selous's zebras, each named after the explorer who first identified the subspecies. The subspecies originally identified by Burchell is now extinct, but the plains zebras as a group are still called Burchell's zebras. All of these zebras stand about 4½ feet (1.37 meters) tall and have wider stripes than the Grévy's or mountain zebra. Punda and the other

zebras in the wildlife park were Grant's zebras.

Even within a subspecies of zebra there is great variety in markings. No two zebras are exactly alike, and the stripes can be used like fingerprints to tell one individual from another.

A fourth kind of zebra, the quagga, had stripes only on its head, neck, and forequarters, and once lived in large herds in South Africa.

It was hunted ruthlessly by early settlers and became extinct in 1883, when the last one, which was living in a zoo in Europe, died. The quagga got its name from the short barking noise that it made, which sounded like "kwa-kwa" or "quagga." Burchell's zebras are closely related to the quagga, and they make the same sound to warn one another that danger is near.

Male zebra

Zebras usually live in small herds of five to twenty animals. In the wildlife park, there were two herds, each with about fifteen animals. The leader of each herd was a full-grown male zebra, and the other members were adult females and their young. The male watched over the females and their offspring and made sure that they stayed together and in one area of the park.

Adult zebras usually stay with the same herd for their whole lives. Herd members do not associate with zebras from any other herd, and females mate only with the herd's leader.

From a distance, male and female zebras look much the same. Both have stocky bodies, short legs, and thick necks topped by a short stiff mane. However, the males, which are called *stallions*, are more muscular and tend to be slightly larger,

Female zebra

weighing up to 700 pounds (318 kilograms). Stallions do not usually mate until they are five or six years old, when they reach their full height and weight.

Females are called *mares* and have a more rounded appearance than males, particularly when they are pregnant or have recently given birth. Female zebras are ready to mate for the first time when they are thirteen months old, although they do not usually become pregnant until the age of two and a half. They can have a baby zebra about once a year after that. Usually, though, they give birth only once every two or three years. A zebra mare is pregnant for slightly more than twelve months. She gives birth to a single baby, which is called a *foal*. A male foal is called a *colt*, and a female foal is called a *filly*.

A newborn foal weighs between 60 and 70 pounds (27–32 kilograms) and stands about 3 feet (1 meter) tall. It is a miniature version of its mother, although its fur is softer and fuzzier, and its stripes are brown-and-tan rather than black-and-white.

Immediately after Punda was born, his mother licked him all over. Then, nudging him gently, she encouraged him to stand. Punda was hungry and needed to stand up to eat.

While his mother stood quietly, Punda searched under her belly until he found one of her two teats. As with all baby mammals, a foal's first food is its mother's milk. During the first week or so, milk was all that Punda would eat or drink. Then he would begin to eat grass like the other zebras. Gradually, as he grew older, the grass would replace milk as his main food. A young zebra grows quickly during its first weeks of life. It must become strong enough to run with the herd without tiring.

During the day, zebras spend most of their time either eating or looking for food. In the wild, their main foods are grass and low-growing plants, although in the dry season they may dig for roots. In the park, the zebras also ate hay that was provided in feeders. To eat, a zebra snips off the grass or hay with sharp front teeth, then chews it with large flat molars. These grinding teeth grow throughout a zebra's life, so they never wear out.

In the wild, zebras often graze side by side with wildebeests, or gnus, and various kinds of antelopes. The zebras prefer to eat tall, coarse grass. The wildebeests like lower-growing, leafy grass, and the antelopes eat small, tender, new grass. Because each animal has a different diet, there is enough food for all.

When many animals graze together, they help protect one another. Each species can recognize the alarm calls of the others. So if one animal senses danger, all will be warned.

As Punda's mother grazed, the colt kept close by her side. When she wanted Punda to move, she gave him a gentle nudge with her head or pushed him with her body. In a few days, Punda would learn to recognize his mother by her scent, stripe pattern, and call. Then he could safely wander away from her for short periods of time.

After birth, as soon as a newborn foal gets to its feet, it instinctively follows the nearest moving object. Usually this is its mother. The mother watches over her newborn carefully, and if any other zebra in the herd comes too close, she chases it away. Even the leader is kept at a distance.

About three days after giving birth, the mare will be ready to mate again. Then she will let the leader approach.

On the African plains, a herd of zebras usually means that there is water nearby. Zebras need to drink water daily and rarely wander far from a water hole.

In Africa, the rainy season normally occurs during the spring and summer months, except near the equator, where there are two shorter rainy seasons each year. When it rains, heavy storms soak the ground every two or three days and keep the water holes filled. But during the six-month dry season that follows, the smaller water holes disappear. Then the zebras migrate to permanent sources of water such as lakes and rivers. When the rainy season returns and the water holes are full, the animals return to the open plains.

Each day, Punda grew bigger and stronger, but he still tired easily as he tried to follow his mother. Sometimes he would lie down and take a nap in the warm summer sun while she quietly grazed nearby.

Adult zebras can sleep standing up, although they, too, often lie down at night to rest. In the wild, zebras rest in open short-grass areas where predators cannot hide. Even so, at least one zebra, usually the stallion that is the leader of the herd, remains standing during the night. He watches to make sure an enemy does not come near. Even when resting, the whole herd must always be ready to take off at a moment's notice.

Punda's mother's long ears turned whenever she heard anything un-usual, and she stopped whatever she was doing until she could determine that there was no danger. If an enemy was detected, either a snort or a sharp barking sound would alert the whole herd. When the herd flees, the zebras all call to one another so that no one becomes lost in the chase. If any zebra does become separated, the others will search until it is found.

Zebras have good eyesight, excellent hearing, and a good sense of smell. A zebra's eyes are set high on either side of its head and allow the zebra a wide range of vision. Even when bending over to eat, a zebra can look out over the tall grass.

Young zebras, which cannot run as fast or as long as older zebras, must take care to stay with the herd, for if they get separated, they can be in great danger. On the African plains, zebras are the main food of lions. The lions wait in the tall grass and spring when a zebra comes close. Choosing an individual that has strayed from the herd, the lion pounces. It bites the zebra's neck and kills it instantly.

After the lion has eaten its fill, other meat-eaters arrive. Hyenas, vultures, and meat-eating insects will pick the carcass clean until only the skeleton remains. Packs of wild dogs also pursue zebras across the plains, working as a team to bring a zebra down. By killing old, sick, and weak animals, predators help keep the zebra herds strong because then the healthiest animals are the ones that are left to breed.

Lions at Masai-Mara National Park in Kenya. In the wild, zebras are an important source of food for lions.

A zebra's main defense against predators is its ability to flee. Zebras have strong, sturdy legs, and their hooves, like those of horses, are ideal for running at high speed over hard-packed ground. They can run for very long distances without tiring or slowing down. Although a newborn zebra's legs are thin, they are nearly as long as those of an adult. From the first day after birth, a young zebra can run with the herd, although only for short distances at first.

Like horses, zebras have three gaits: walking, trotting, and galloping. When walking, each foot moves separately in an even rhythm, whereas in trotting, diagonal pairs of feet move together. Galloping is a complicated sequence in which all four feet are off the ground at the same time once in each stride. A zebra can gallop at speeds of up to 37 miles (60 kilometers) per hour.

As Punda grew older, the young zebra's brown fuzzy coat gradually became smoother and the stripes more clearly defined. Soon all his stripes would be black-and-white, like those of the other zebras.

For a long time, people have argued about whether zebras are white animals with black stripes or black animals with white stripes. Today most scientists agree that they are white with black stripes.

People have also wondered why zebras have stripes, since the stripes do not appear to help them hide from their enemies. Out in the open, the zebra's black-and-white pattern makes the zebra stand out clearly against grass or sky. However, the uneven spacing of the stripes makes the edge of the zebra's shape harder to see, and this may confuse predators, especially when the zebra is moving. If a hunter, such as a lion, is confused for even a second, it could save the zebra's life.

By the age of four months, Punda's muscles had gotten much stronger, and his body was filling out. As he became more sure of himself, he no longer needed to stay with his mother all the time. Often he joined the other young zebras in the herd. Like all baby animals, they enjoyed playing with one another. Sometimes they pushed and shoved each other in play fights. Other times they raced across the park, seemingly just for the fun of running fast. For young zebras in the wild, these games help them learn skills needed to survive as adults.

When the zebras in the wildlife park were not eating or resting, they were grooming themselves and one another. Using their tongues and teeth, they cleaned their coats. They pulled out burrs or scratched insect bites. For itches that could not be scratched with a foot or rubbed on a tree or a fence post, the zebras liked to roll on the ground.

Wherever there are horses, there are usually insects, and the zebra's tail is a good flyswatter. On hot afternoons, when insects were swarming, every tail in the herd seemed to be in constant motion.

In the wild, when a filly is ready to mate for the first time, several stallions from outside the herd may approach her. The stallion that is the leader of her herd will try to prevent these other males from coming near. First he will challenge each rival with lips pulled back and teeth bared. This warning may be enough to make the other stallion leave. If not, a fight may develop.

A zebra male has four more teeth than a zebra female. These extra teeth, which are in the front of the mouth, are sharp and can be used to inflict a nasty bite.

Often, while the stallion is fighting one zebra, another male that has been waiting on the sidelines takes his chance to mate with the filly. She will follow him and stay with him unless the stallion from her original herd fights to get her back. In this way, a young male is sometimes able to steal away a young mare from another herd and start his own herd. A filly either becomes a permanent member of her mother's herd or leaves to go with a new stallion at about the age of two and a half.

In the wild, when two herds of zebras meet, the stallions greet one another by sniffing and touching each other. In the park, these meetings often developed into small skirmishes. At first the two zebras paced, side by side, along an invisible line that divided the areas where their herds were grazing. As the stallions approached and sniffed each other, their actions seemed to say, "Stay away from my herd or you'll be sorry."

Usually their conflicts were limited to pushing and shoving, but sometimes a full-scale battle erupted, with kicking and biting. The winner then demonstrated his victory by chasing the other zebra back to his own area.

By the time Punda was seven months old, he no longer needed to drink his mother's milk and his only food was grass and hay. In captivity, a fully grown zebra can eat the equivalent of 20 pounds (9 kilograms) of hay a day, as well as other food supplements. Although Punda now weighed about 300 pounds (136 kilograms) and was about half-grown, he still stayed with his mother most of the time.

In the wild, a colt stays with the herd until he is about three years old. Usually by then his mother has a new foal to look after. Then the colt leaves to join a bachelor herd of other young males. If he gets the chance, he may try to steal a female and start his own herd. A young stallion may also challenge an older stallion that already has a herd. If they fight and the young stallion wins, he will take over the whole herd. Usually stallions are not strong enough to establish and keep their own female herd until they are at least five years old.

An older stallion that has lost his herd will join a bachelor herd, where he will stay for the rest of his life. Because there is no bachelor herd in the wildlife park, young males like Punda are often traded or sold to zoos or other parks when they become old enough to mate. Sometimes they replace older stallions, and sometimes they start new herds.

Zebras like Punda can look forward to a long and healthy life in zoos and animal parks. Zebras in captivity often live into their twenties, and several in zoos have reached the age of twenty-eight, a long life-span for any member of the horse family.

Huge herds of zebras were a common sight for early explorers in Africa. Because it seemed as if there was an endless supply of wildlife, little care was taken to protect the animals. Yet today many of the herds are gone, and some species, such as the quagga, have become extinct. Most of the animals that are left live in areas where they are protected from hunters.

The zebras' home is one of the most magnificent wildlife areas in the world, but it is constantly shrinking as cities and farms grow. Nowhere else is there such a rich variety or so many large animals. This land and the animals that live on it are a valuable resource that can never be replaced. We must take care to preserve it for future generations so they, too, can know the beautiful striped horses of the African plains.

INDEX

Photographs are in **boldface.**